Embracing Me

by,
DeLana Rutherford

Embracing Me

Copyright © 2017 DeLana Rutherford

Scripture references included in this book are from the King James Version and New King James Version of the Bible.

Books can be ordered through booksellers or by contacting:

DeLana Rutherford
1635 Old 41 Hwy NW
Suite 112-210
Kennesaw, GA 30152

ISBN-13: 978-0692891346 (Level Three Worship)
ISBN-10: 069289134X

DEDICATION

I am so excited to dedicate this book to some very special people in my life!

First of all, GOD! I thank Him for never giving up on me. Jesus Christ, I'm so thankful for Your love, grace and mercy. For every conviction that I carry in my heart that keeps me going and on the right path...I love you!

My man! Myles Rutherford, the love of my life! When I say, you are the real thing, I mean it! Your love for me, your guidance, your patience and support are evident and without rival! Thank you!

My children – Brooklyn, you are one of the main reasons why I keep pushing every day to be a better woman. I want you to love who you are more every day. You are a jewel and a rare find. I love you!

Lyncoln, my favorite boy in the world! You are so unique and so very special to me. Your future is so bright and we are waiting on you to unveil all it has. I love you!

My parents and pastors, Joseph and Yolanda Morgan. Thank you for staying true to God and showing me what it looks like to stand, no matter what. I love you both.

Worship with Wonders Church family, your love and support is obvious. It's so constant and true. We are family and I love you all!

Now, last but not least! My be YOU on purpose movement – how this has changed my life! It started so simple and has grown to be such a statement all over the world, changing so many lives. I'm so thankful that this statement left my mouth one day and now has become such a movement impacting all of us. The greatest moments are still to come. Thank you to all who have believed in this and joined me.

Thank you to every person who purchases this book for you and others. May it make a difference in your life like it has mine.

TABLE OF CONTENTS

Introduction

Chapter 1..House of Mirrors

Chapter 2..Love Beyond Emotions

Chapter 3..Rejection Bully

Chapter 4..Who Will I Be Today?

Chapter 5........Paralyzing Depression/I Can't Breathe Anxiety

Chapter 6..Strong Woman

Chapter 7..STOP! DROP! LISTEN!

Chapter 8..Defining Moments

Chapter 9..Letter from the First Lady

Chapter 10.. Pastor of Alabaster

INTRODUCTION

This whole book is about Embracing Me and hopefully helping others to do the same. I share personal stories, challenges and victories that I have experienced. My prayer is that it encourages every reader to embrace who God has created them to be, to learn to love the process of life and to gain in every season. Embracing me doesn't mean I don't acknowledge my flaws and mistakes. It just means that I'm learning to embrace me as I make the changes that I can and realize that it's part of the journey. There will always be things we don't like, but that doesn't mean we give up. Learn to love you.

The word Embrace means:

to hold someone in your arms as a way of expressing love or friendship.

As we begin to embrace ourselves, it's much easier to embrace others. This doesn't mean we become arrogant or self-absorbent. It just means we finally accept our God-given identity and we are proud to embrace it and live it with confidence.

I pray you enjoy reading every story and simple words of advice in this book. It's changing my life. I'm thankful that He is revealing my purpose in life every day!

HOUSE OF MIRRORS

As a child, I remember going to the State Fair every year with my family. They always had this thing called the "House of Mirrors". Do you remember those? It was always fun to go in because you could change what you looked like just by standing in front of a mirror. The mirror wasn't magic, it just had the ability to make you look like something or someone else. They had so many different ones. One to make you taller, one to make you shorter, skinnier, thicker, whatever you wanted. It lasted just a moment, but those who thought they were too tall, got to see what it would be like to be short. I think you get the picture of what I am saying. I would watch many people stand in front of those mirrors and laugh, get quiet and most just play it off that it was just a joke. Truthfully, many wished they could make it come true.

So many women hate looking in the mirror. It has become one of their greatest fears and they dread to see themselves. We constantly want to change the person staring back at us. We have become so negative over our looks that it has made us miserable. We have to do better!

Who do you see? What do you see? Whether others have told us negative things about ourselves or we have put them on ourselves, this is a real issue with women especially. We see words like, ugly, fat, not worthy, shame, guilt, too old, I wish I could change this or that, no one will ever see me without makeup and the list goes on and on. Our words are powerful. Everything that was formed, first started with words. What we say is what we get and what we begin to believe.

Every time you look in the mirror and label negative words over yourself, you are insulting the masterpiece that He calls perfect. When He created you, He made no mistakes! He knew you before you were in your mother's womb. How can that not be a miracle of a masterpiece? He loved us all enough to make us each as individuals. He was creative and specific in all of His plans and desires for each one of us. I can't imagine how He feels each time we look in the mirror and discredit and discount what He sees as an amazing wonder.

When I turned 40 I felt like I was already days from 50! My mind tried to tell me I couldn't do certain things or dress like me (which is very eclectic). I saw wrinkles that were totally unwelcomed and new gray hair that I did not feel showed wisdom. I knew botox was available, but maybe my denial stopped that from happening. Either way, I was getting older and I had to find a way to embrace that and be happy about it! Nothing in me wanted to relive my younger days, but boy was I missing that smooth face, lifted buttocks and you probably know the rest of the list since it's on yours too. I mean, did God really mean for us to have our own private summer with these hot flashes? I'm looking for cute fans now more than cute shoes because I can't walk in my old 4-inch heels anyway!

Life doesn't stop so we have to find the beauty and humor in each stage. My goal is to look in the mirror, even on my worst days and say, 'Girl, you are beautiful!' If I catch myself seeing or saying something different, I have started asking God to forgive me. It's like giving our children something that cost us everything, thinking it is amazing and them bringing it to us multiple times a day saying how much they hate it, how ugly it is and they don't want it because they want what others have more. Can you imagine how heartbreaking and insulting that would be? He made each of us in His image. He made no mistakes. We must begin to appreciate and value that.

5

When we look in the mirror, we must see what He calls valuable and irreplaceable. We must start our day by seeing our worth. When the thoughts begin to flood our mind, we must replace them with compliments. We must take inventory of why we think like we do. You are precious to your creator. You are irreplaceable to Him. He spent time on creating you just like He wanted you to be. As the inner man heals, the outer man becomes a precious beauty that cannot be duplicated. We have to begin to see the things around us that truly matter. Our bodies and faces will change, but the beauty inside remains. We have to get to a place where we decide that we have something to offer. We are courageous, strong women that make a difference. If you stop to think about it, to be consumed with our outer bodies is pretty petty and self-consumed. This doesn't mean we have to take things to the extreme and hate make-up, hate looking nice and be against taking care of ourselves. Women like pretty things and that is great! Let's just find balance and place value on the things that mean the most. Once you do this, you begin to enjoy life so much more.

Wake up each morning and live by these words,
I am fearfully and wonderfully made.

Girl....YOU ARE BEAUTIFUL!

LOVE BEYOND EMOTIONS

Why do we spend so much time thinking and talking about the negatives in life? It does nothing but steal our time, our peace, our joy and our future. Tell me what's good about that! The facts are, sometimes life SUCKS! Yes, I said it! I hate that word, but sometimes it's very fitting. We can't control everything that happens. Neither can we control others' actions, but we can control ours. We have to do better at not letting people push our buttons so easily. We focus so much on what others are doing or not doing, that we lose focus on what we could be doing. My husband says this all of the time, "My haters are not my motivators...they are my prayer assignment." What would happen if more of us got that revelation and actually started praying for those who are against us or have done us wrong?

People will come and go and we have to stop taking it so personal. I know, sometimes it's family that pushes our buttons more than what seems to be a real enemy. We have to learn to celebrate the differences in one another and embrace that not everyone will agree with how we do life.

I personally love very hard. When I care about someone, I genuinely care about them. There have been many times that I have helped people with no strings attached, but assuming that they would at least appreciate it. I have found over the years of my life that if we are not careful, we will expect others' reactions to be dictated on our level of thinking or how we have been raised to respond. Let me explain that a little better.

Sometimes the people that we are assigned to assist in life are called to us for a season or a reason. Not everyone that you pour into is meant to be close to you for the rest of your life. This was a really hard fact for me to accept. When I gave my time, my love, my money, my heart to them, I expected a lot back. I expected everyone to be lifers...people that stay close to you for life. God had to really deal with me to show me that not everyone was raised like me and not everyone would respond how I thought they should. This doesn't mean that it's okay, it just means that it's true. We have opened our home to teenagers that have walked away and crushed our hearts at times. It hurt our children and left them, as well as us, wanting to put up a wall that would never be torn down again. It made us want to question who we were, what we stood for and so many other thoughts and emotions. You have moments of being sad, angry, numb and so much more.

I remember taking a shower one day and telling God, "I'm done with this certain individual". God spoke back to me and said, "You don't get to make that decision". He proceeded to tell me, "...just like I never said I was done with you". I didn't really know how to respond to that. I just stood there and said, "Okay God". See, when God assigns people to our lives, it has purpose. Not just for them, but for us too. He never asked us to get stepped on or taken advantage of and I don't believe we have to sign up for that. However, we don't get to make the decision to walk away if He hasn't released us to walk away. Some people take longer than others to get it. Sometimes some people never get it. Those are the times we may have to face the fact that the lesson was for us and not them. I used to think a few of the ones we were there for didn't receive anything and that we did it all for nothing and no results. God quickly showed me and reminded me of the scripture and I want to remind you that, one sows, one waters, but He gives the increase. Even though we want to say we will never love like that again or allow anyone in our close space again, we know in order to love like Christ, we must keep loving too.

Once we give all we have to those He has called us to, we have to keep them at His feet and trust that whenever and however He chooses, that they will come full circle and He will finish what He started in them. The more you pray for them and tell God you release the emotions attached, the more He takes over and reveals His perfect plan. Not just for them, but for you too. It's a beautiful thing.

So many of us circle the same mountain and same problem because we are too emotional or too stubborn to let go of what we can't change or fix. Emotions can make you sick! We have to stop letting others occupy so much space in our minds. I call them "fruit killers". Whatever you think, so shall you be. Whatever has your mind, has your heart. Whatever has your heart, has your time. We need to constantly remind ourselves of the important things in life. We do not get to choose our tests, but we do choose our battles. Choose wisely. After each test, you should always be able to look back and see what you have learned. Some tests we have failed, but thank God for more chances to get it right.

I want to challenge you to open your heart and ask God to continue to put people in your life that you can help along their journey. All through this book you will hear about let downs, victories and lessons. Life will always have all three of those and that's also why I titled this book "Embracing Me", because even in those times in my life, I must remember who I am and embrace every mistake and every triumph. I must learn that this is my journey and it was created for me to follow out in my own skin. The next time you want to give up on someone, remember, He never gave up on you and He never will! We must continue to love like Christ or we are living in vain. Every time we are hurt or rejected, we must realize that it isn't the person, it's the root that they haven't dealt with. A lot of people are not used to being loved. Maybe that's you. I want to encourage you to open your heart. Allow people in that are qualified to love you and walk with you through life. No one is perfect and we will always make mistakes, but having someone that really cares about you in this thing called life makes it much easier. Always remember, before you judge anyone's now, don't forget they have a past just like you. Maybe they haven't healed yet. You can be a part of that process. Care genuinely and love with no reserve. No strings attached...just a heart like His and know He has the last say. When we choose to love beyond our carnal ability, we are beginning to be more like our God. Keep in mind how many times He has forgiven you and begin to grace others. Remember that love is a choice, not an emotion. Emotions will mess you up, but choices will direct your future. Choose wisely!

REJECTION BULLY

One of my biggest issues I had to overcome was trying to please everyone. I grew up as a pastors' daughter and felt as if all eyes were on me no matter what I did. I felt like I was on a pedestal and everyone was watching my every move. I tried to be the good daughter with low maintenance and just stay out of the way as much as possible. No, I was never perfect, but I was exhausted trying to be. Trying to fit in and trying to be a people pleaser will wear you out. You will never satisfy them all, while you remain empty trying.

I will never forget a certain day when I was about 31 years old. I prayed for so many people in the altars of our church to where they almost had to carry me out to my office afterward. I asked everyone to leave my office and I fell to my knees to thank God for using me and just to spend a few moments with Him. What happened next was not expected. I began to go through deliverance right there by myself. I cried out to God and said, "I'm used to this with others, but what is this about for me?" It scared me to where I began to ask God to send my husband in there with me. He did and when Myles walked in, I fell in his arms and told him what was happening. Later I asked the Lord, 'What was that about?' He began to reveal to me that He was delivering me from years of rejection. Rejection? What? I didn't even realize that I was dealing with rejection. I didn't know that I had let things build up on the inside of me and it was affecting my health, my mind and the way I was responding to others.

My parents grew up in the church and are incredible people, pastors and parents. For years, I watched my parents navigate through pastoring and life, on call 24-7 and having two older brothers that were addicted to drugs in their teen years and even after. They loved us all and gave their lives for God and their children. But in the process of trying to save my brothers, even though they loved me and were amazing parents, I had begun to feel rejected and didn't even realize it. Many people wonder how that could happen and that may seem small to some, but as a teenager, it was real for me, whatever it was. So many hours were spent helping others, traveling and trying to keep up with the demands people put on them.

It wasn't just this situation where I felt rejection. I felt like because I was shy when I was younger, that I never fit in. I later realized there was much more to this. The day I laid it all down in my office, I felt like a new woman. I felt as if God came in that room and told me He loved me enough to take me back years ago to reveal a root that had grown in my heart and spirit. My dad always taught me, whatever you magnify will manifest. I had created some of it in my mind that everyone was against me, no one liked me like I was, I didn't offer what others could and so much more. In my mind, I even thought at times that if I didn't have a crazy drug story or tell every negative detail that happened to me, who would listen? I started to believe what the enemy was whispering and sometimes shouting in my ears. Again, whether it was true or not, it was real to me. I had to confront what had been bullying me, either way. Sometimes you have to face the fear of going back to heal what was never dealt with. So many times we would rather ignore the pain or try to cover it with temporary fixes, but until we are willing to confront it, we will never conquer it. Our thoughts can hold us hostage, steal from us and even control our daily lives if we allow them to. Our thoughts are powerful and dictate our actions.

The word says, "Whatever things are true, whatever things are noble, whatever things are just, whatever things are pure, whatever things are lovely and of good report - think on these things." – Philippians 4:8

It has been a very challenging journey some days, but so rewarding when you begin to see progress and freedom. You will find a new joy and a purpose in your life and begin to recognize it in others that you can now help in their process. In the 'church world', many tell you not to tell your story because people will judge you or think less of you, on and on. How are we to help others if we can't be transparent ourselves? People on the pews or chairs are not fooled any longer. They are screaming out for help and if we ignore what we need to work on ourselves, we are all in trouble. People want something real. They want to know that someone has been through what they are going through and they made it. They need hope and comfort that they will get through their process. How will they hear if we don't speak? Religious people will always tell you to keep it to yourself to protect your reputation, but I read in the word that it says, you win them over by the blood of the Lamb and the word of your testimony. Telling your story frees you and others! Telling your story doesn't mean you have to stay stuck in that bondage, it just means it doesn't hold you hostage any longer.

This is a poem I wrote several years ago:

"Too Long in a Box"

Too long not loving what I see
Unsatisfied with status quo
Pleasing everyone
While losing the real me

No longer would I sit back
Be fake, be hurt, be quiet
I had to heal...this was real...
Something had to change

I found HIM, I found ME
Realized I was purchased and regardless...
Would be ME on purpose
Be happy, be free,

bo YOU on purpoзc

WHO WILL I BE TODAY?

The world and society today makes no apologies for the corrupt images they have seduced the female gender with. It no longer just exists in the world, but has made its way very blatantly into the church as well. For some reason, it is hard for the younger females especially, to understand that most of the photos they see on social media or plastered in their faces on magazines are fine, airbrush work or great edits by the click of a button. Those same females have the same struggles we all face. They have cellulite, acne breakouts, bad hair days and many things they don't like when they face the mirror. I see girls all the time on social media who have created so many edits on their picture that they are almost unrecognizable. WE WANT TO SEE THE REAL YOU!

There's always a tug-of-war to want to be you and then be another. Comparison can be such an ugly struggle. When you continue to compare yourself to others you will never find the real you because the real you never gets the chance to express itself when you stay in comparison mode.

I often tell a story about a young lady that was in my life for many years. She was young, beautiful, gifted, anointed and so much more. I walked with her through several seasons of life and counted her as a friend. One evening we were at church for an event and she approached me saying, "I need to talk to you tonight", so I met with her in an office at the church. As we sat there and she began to be transparent with me, I was blown away at how she felt about me. I have always had a huge respect for honesty and hate being lied to, so she already had my attention just by finally coming to me to speak what she had been feeling in all honesty. She began to tell me that she was very jealous of me. She said, "How can you dress like you do with confidence? How can you wear that hat you have on now and pull it off? You sing, you are petite...", on and on. To be honest, I sat there in shock because I really didn't know it was that deep. I was hurt, confused, mad and felt very awkward at the same time. As I listened to her, I had to quickly think about my response. I had a moment to get it together inside before I let my flesh get the best of me. Part of me wanted to really let her have it. How dare her? God quickly dealt with me and I had to see the real issue here. Instead of adding to her insecurity by rejecting her true feelings, I embraced her. I begin to tell her how beautiful she was and wanted to encourage her to overcome the lies the enemy had her believing. It ended well and God continued to restore that situation.

The Bible says to love your neighbor as you love yourself. Think about that. So many women can't love others because they can't even love themselves. They are so caught up in others' lives that they never experience their own. There is so much God is wanting us to enjoy in life and we are too caught up comparing. If we would learn to stop and evaluate what we do have and count the blessings in our lives, we would see that there is so much more to be thankful for.

The Bible says in Song of Solomon 8:6, Set me as a seal upon your heart, as a seal upon your arm; For love is as strong as death, jealousy as cruel as the grave; Its flames are flames of fire, a most vehement flame." The word vehement means, marked by forceful energy, intensely emotional; deeply felt; bitterly.

Jealousy and bitterness are so cruel. They rip families apart, they destroy relationships and send so many to their graves. So many mothers have never confronted their demons of these two evil monsters. Therefore, they are just handed down, generation after generation. They only become stronger for the next little girl coming up. If more women would see the dangers and reckless behavior that jealousy and bitterness create and stop to be delivered from them, we would see a lot more freedom in the generations behind us. It only takes one to see enough of the damage and be determined that it stops with them. We reap what we sow. We must stop daily and ask ourselves, what am I sowing. See, so many women feel as if something is owed to them because of what they have been through. Many feel as if, I can't forgive because they don't deserve that. They feel like if they forgive someone, it's condoning their actions. It's not! It's actually setting the victim free. Whatever is holding you bound by jealousy and bitterness, let it go! Right now, while you are reading this, set this book down a moment and let it go! Let them go! Your health, your peace and your joy are more important than what happened to you. You will find love for yourself and grace for others when you let it go.

In order for us to love others, we must find reasons to love ourselves. This isn't ego, it's confidence. Stop to list the great things about yourself. He made you so unique and

24

just like He wanted you. Face you and begin to love! It is okay to love yourself.

We have to stop competing with someone we will never be. We can't be someone that He didn't create. It is not even possible. So stop going in circles and trying to find someone different. We are equipped to be who we are created to be. You can't produce what you are not. A lot of women never feel fulfilled in who they are or their passion because they never stop trying to be someone else. You can't fulfill your purpose when you are not on your own journey. When you are not in your lane, it's a dangerous road that leads to dead ends. You stay frustrated and never satisfied. Your purpose should always make you happy even on the hard days. You will find strength to keep going when it's your passion. Your purpose should always bless you and others!

Make a decision and a commitment to yourself to discover the real you. Start by living out your passion in everyday life. So many people make finding their purpose so complicated. It isn't! Find what you love to do and make it a lifelong dream that you live out daily to accomplish. Make time to think about your passions. List them out and start small by making small goals that you can achieve. You have to be realistic, but full of faith. Work as if you have to do it all and pray as if God has to do it all. When you discover what you love, you will discover your passion. When you discover your passion, you discover your purpose. When you discover your purpose, you begin to live out your destiny. This is where true fulfillment happens.

So start by saying a prayer. Ask God to forgive you if you need to. Continue to pray for those who have wronged you and let them go. Write down the things you do love about yourself. Begin to discover your passions that may have been buried in the grave. Resurrect your faith in yourself and begin on a fresh, new journey to discover the real you. If you have already done all of these things, begin to find others that may need your help. You will find the most fulfillment when you are helping others.

PARALYZING DEPRESSION/I CAN'T BREATHE ANXIETY

Depression doesn't give you a heads-up and is no respecter of persons. It is an uninvited darkness that paralyzes you.

I went through depression in 2007 after moving to Atlanta with my family to start our church. My husband, Myles, myself and our 2 amazing children, Brooklyn and Lyncoln. We were very busy and before I knew it, I found myself staying sick with a weakened immune system. I was trying to keep up with being a wife, a mom and a pastor of people I didn't even know. We worked nonstop to get the church going. We started in a movie theater where we were unloading and reloading a trailer every week while setting up in Community Centers during the week. We later found a building that was 27,000 square feet that rocked our world. It was a miracle how that happened. God performed a miracle for us! They told us it would be $25,000.00 a month and by the time we were done, God brought it down to $2,500.00 a month. We still didn't know where that was coming from, but we knew to take it! We had to renovate the whole place. We went through sewage floods to you name it in that building. We ripped out stages, stripped nails from old wood, because we didn't have money to buy new. We knew God sent us to Atlanta and we were in pursuit. But I was exhausted!

I became sick one day (again) so I went to the local Minute Clinic near our home. They prescribed me with steroids, Z-packs, etc. I went home, sat on the couch and took the pills. Before I knew it, I was laying on the floor of our living room convulsing from anxiety. My body was reacting to the pills that were pretty much shutting down the rest of the adrenals that I had left. I rolled over and grabbed my cell phone in one hand and my house phone in the other to call for help. Myles was at the church and beat the two ambulance trucks in our driveway. I called 911 and tried to tell them where I was, but I kept speaking in tongues. I'm sure they thought maybe I was speaking Spanish. When they finally got me to the hospital, I was trembling all over and really felt as if I was going to die on that floor that day. My body and my mind began to shut down on me rapidly. I was leading worship weekly and could barely stand. I dropped down to 97 pounds and thought I was losing my mind for real. I remember one day looking out of a big window in our bathroom and telling God, 'If this is how I have to live, please take me'. I didn't want my husband to live with me like I was. Our children were young at the time, but I had so much guilt when I didn't have the strength to play with them or engage mentally. I was so deep into depression. I was in and out of the hospital with anxiety night after night. I wouldn't let my husband leave my side because of fear that I would stop breathing. My parents came to pick me up to get me away for the weekend and I remember my mother sitting on the floor by the couch, begging me to eat. I had no desire for anything! She began to feed me chicken broth in a spoon and packed me up for Nashville. My husband stayed home to preach that Sunday and then drove to Nashville to pick me up after service. I will never forget getting in the shower and hearing them laugh downstairs as they enjoyed breakfast. They were so full of life. I got out of the shower and went downstairs and yelled, 'Somebody get me some help!' I couldn't do it another day! My mother called her kinesiologist and they brought me in. He began to test me and diagnosed me with adrenal exhaustion. So many people have this and have no idea, just like I didn't. I was just glad to hear that I could get better.

Every day for the next several months, my husband would tell me, "You are going to be okay!" I am a praying woman, but we have to remember that some things have to be done in the natural as well. I was taken off of all caffeine, sugar and bread immediately and was recommended to go to a bio identical hormone specialist. As soon as I returned home, I did this right way. Although it took strict food changes, stress evaluation and life changes, I started getting better on about a 6-month journey. There were hard days, but I had to make the decision to save myself before I could assist in saving everyone else. I refused to live a stressed out life. Life was busy, sometimes people left the church that broke my heart, but I still had to live. I put God and family back in the top priorities of my life and the rest could fall in order after that. A lot of times we want to blame the devil for what we are going through and no doubt, he is to blame for a lot, but some things we must change ourselves.

Depression and anxiety are real. If you have ever experienced either one, you know most of the time, they go together. They take away from your social abilities and rob you of so much. I do believe a lot of females have hormonal imbalances and this can cause so many negatives in our lives if we don't get them in check. We must go to the source of the issue before we just decide to throw pills down our throats, that most of the time make it worse. I am not a doctor and I am not telling anyone to trash their pills. I was a victim and I know what worked for me. I made a shirt for my boutique that says, "Depression and anxiety suck, but I conquered it!" Maybe it is a daily fight for some, but whatever you do, don't stop fighting. Don't hide it thinking it will just go away on its own either. Do something to get healthy help.

What good are we if we lose ourselves, our peace and almost our mind? We have to be good for ourselves, then for someone else. We have to find a balance and have some non-negotiables for ourselves. Our children will imitate what we do and say, so we must find the positives in the daily hustle. Learn when to walk away and breathe for a few moments. I don't always make time for the gym, but I do make time to sit and reflect on the good things, scroll through inspiring Instagram posts, eat an apple on the porch or my favorite chair with fresh ground almond butter that I love. It's the simple things in life that will always keep us grounded. We don't really need what we think we need to make us happy. Discover what makes you smile and what drives you to true peace and do that more. Choose your battles and recognize what is and isn't worth your time. Celebrate those who celebrate you! We are all given a time to live on this earth, live it with peace and joy. So many people spend more time rehearsing who left them, who hurt them, who did them wrong, on and on, more than they think about who has stayed with them, fought for them and who is pushing them to win. If you are breathing, you still have life. Live it with happiness.

STRONG WOMAN

I grew up in church and have been around strong preachers and leaders all of my life. I was born in New Orleans, Louisiana, which I love and also have a little trace of Spanish genes in me. All that to say, I am spicy, know what I want and go after it with full force. As a child, I knew what I wanted and I never liked "no" for an answer. In my teen years, I was strong, but more reserved in certain areas. I didn't like singing or talking in front of anyone. I had to be pushed to be out front. I was in a relationship my senior year that was not healthy for me. My parents encouraged me very strongly to attend World Harvest Bible College for a short season. My dad told me, "I think you should go for six months and you may meet your husband". I packed my bags and moved to Ohio for five months.

He was right...I found him and I was so thankful! I called my parents one night and said, "Start praying because I have found my husband". He was unlike anyone I had ever dated. I knew it was God! He was beyond my dreams and still is. We got married in 1996 and now have two wonderful children, Brooklyn and Lyncoln. When we got married, he moved to Tennessee so he could work out of my parents' church with me. We did everything we could get our hands on in ministry. We served as Youth Pastors for nine years, with the Dance Ministry, Outreach, bussing in over 90 kids from the projects weekly and I was the receptionist as well. We loved it all and wanted to do it all. We had no idea what God was preparing us for. We thought we were going to travel the world and sing after all of that. After about ten years of marriage, my husband came to me and said, "Baby, God is calling us to pastor". I said, 'I'm sorry, but you are crazy!' I saw my parents go through too much! I wanted to travel and sing with our children. I told God that if this was Him, to please prick my heart and to please speak to me too. He did. I called my mom one day and said, "Mom, I don't want to do this!" She said, "Baby, I would love to tell you to put your tennis shoes on and RUN", but as she broke down and cried, she said, "You will never be able to get away from this". When you are chosen, you won't be happy doing anything else. After that day, the passion was birthed and on my worst days, I have never regretted it. I never signed up to do this, He chose me, therefore He equipped me and I will always be able to do it.

You are probably wondering why the title of this chapter is Strong Woman. It's because I want to talk to you about being one. After the initial shock settled and I accepted what God was calling us to do, about three years later, we were thirty years old. We moved to Kentucky for one year to be with my husband's family before settling down to pastor. We had no idea where we wanted to pastor, but we were seeking God. God kept showing us Atlanta everywhere we turned. We thought it would be too big and there were too many churches already, but God confirmed and with just us four and our dog, we sold our home, most of our possessions and set out to pastor people we had never met. What a scary, but exciting time for us all! We went on a lot of faith and a vision and He met us.

There is so much to this story, but I won't go into all of it. What I want to get to is, we started our church in Regal Cinema Theater. Within the first year, we lived in an apartment that caught on fire, our son was a preemie and couldn't be around smoke and the neighbor smoked like a freight train and it filtered through our walls. The first Sunday, we had over seventy people show up, but most were friends and family from different states and a few locals that saw our billboard or fliers all over town. We were thankful. Then that next Sunday, we had 12 and like I've said before, they were not the 12 Disciples (well maybe some were similar to Judas)...Lord, it's just the truth. About five years into the ministry, we had five other churches start down the road from us in one year, from within our congregation and none were blessed by us. It was so heartbreaking and what we thought we had built for five years, looked as if it was failing. One day my husband was preaching and said, "You have to pray and bless your enemies". He stopped and told God, "I have to do that myself". The day we did that, our church doubled in one summer. We had to forgive those people. Not just the ones who started the churches, but also the ones who followed them. God restored us and taught us so much through every bit of that.

One of hardest things that I had to hear and be healed from was several of them leaving because they said we had no love and I was a Jezebel. My heart broke as I put my head on my desk one day telling God how my heart was aching. It literally was physically hurting. People can say such cruel things. It's easy to say ignore it, but we are human and words do hurt. It set me back for the next year. It tried to shut me down as I was constantly thinking, *what do they think about me,* every time my strong woman came out. I am very clear in my stance and my convictions. When I counsel people, I hold nothing back because He holds me accountable for all I say and how I lead.

One day I was asked to be in a magazine for an amazing pastor, Gayla Bagwell. As they interviewed me, the strong woman vs. Jezebel came to me. God began to show me the difference and it began to free me once again. A Jezebel wants to control who's in charge. She does things behind the scenes that causes chaos as she hides when it hits the roof. She's sneaky, controlling, manipulating and so much more. A strong woman knows who she is, doesn't need to control because she's too busy pushing others and celebrating them. She's confident in herself even though she fails at times. She admits her faults and fixes them. She takes ownership of her life. She supports those around her instead of manipulating and tearing them down. She knows how to compliment others that have more than her and less as well. She protects those she loves and is proud to do so. I could go on and on. On the days I question myself, I go back to this check list. Which one are you? People will always try to label a strong woman as a Jezebel. It's usually the ones who are in denial of who they really are.

If you or someone you know is a Jezebel, begin to pray. They are the most insecure women and need prayer.

I am forever grateful for Him showing me the difference. I am proud to be a Strong Woman!

STOP! DROP! LISTEN!

STOP trying to meet all of the deadlines. Life seems to make us think that we have all of these deadlines that have to be met NOW. If we would STOP and prioritize a daily list, we would be able to accomplish a lot more and feel as if we are actually getting the important things done. STOP waiting until the last minute to achieve small tasks. Planning ahead will eliminate so many frustrations. STOP trying to keep up with everyone else around you. This will wear you out...not just physically, but also mentally. STOP feeling like you don't have what it takes. STOP letting the enemy push you around and knock you down. STOP thinking your dreams will never happen. STOP being a victim. STOP comparing yourself to everyone else. STOP saying you are ugly, not good enough, too old, too fat, too skinny. STOP complaining. STOP talking negative about yourself and others. STOP gossiping and start bragging on others. STOP listening to voices that paralyze your motivation. STOP thinking it's someone else's fault and take ownership. STOP waiting on someone else to make your dreams happen.

DROP the things that can wait. DROP the people that only drain you. DROP the pressure that life tries to put on you. DROP the thoughts that make you feel like you can never accomplish anything. DROP the negative outlook the enemy tries to paint for you. DROP the negative outlook on life. DROP the weights that drag you down. DROP the emotions that keep you on a rollercoaster. DROP unforgiveness. This will free you. You only keep yourself bound and sick when you hold it in. DROP the lies.

LISTEN to your body. Make the commitment to take time for yourself. LISTEN when you feel overwhelmed. Take a moment and regain clarity. LISTEN to your gut. It never lies or steers you wrong. LISTEN to your spirit. It will guide you. LISTEN to God...the first time. Don't second guess His voice. His children know His voice. LISTEN to your leaders. The Bible says, for this will benefit you. LISTEN to what's important. Don't waste time discussing things that don't matter. LISTEN to the voices that increase the quality of your life. LISTEN to those that have made investments in you! Not just with money, but with time or by example. LISTEN to those who have been there. LISTEN to those who have paid a price so you don't have to pay it. LISTEN when your flesh is screaming.

DEFINING MOMENTS

A defining moment is when an event or situation happens in your life and you make the decision to run or embrace it. All of us go through defining moments that can make or break us. We can refrain or reign. We can withdraw or engage. These are the moments where we are being trained. These are the times He is developing our purpose. We can kick, scream, cuss or buck, but these are moments that really define who we are.

Every flaw and every mistake becomes a scar with a story. We can never go back and change what might have happened to us. We can't go back and reverse the bad choices we have made. We can't rewind the past and make every crooked place straight, but we can ask God to use our past to help others. He can use our past to teach us. It's only when we get stuck in our past that our past becomes our present and sometimes even our future. God is not interested in punishing us. He's also not waiting on us to fail again. He's a God full of grace and mercy with lots of love for us all. Think about the worst thing you have ever faced, been through or experienced and know that someone else has been through worse. I know that is hard to understand for many because some of our messes were ugly, but He still loves you, me and them the same.

Just like the woman at the well. Try to imagine how disqualified, full of shame and guilt she must have felt. If she would have let all of her past sins stop her that day, she would have missed her life-changing moment with Jesus. She could have let her pride stop her, but I believe she must have been to the point in life that she was desperate for a change. She knew what she had been doing obviously wasn't working. She recognized a defining moment and took a chance in order to be free. She was the very one that won many others over, because in spite of what the city knew about her, she wanted to tell everyone of man she met that set her free.

Just like David. He always had a heart of worship, but he messed up so many times. God knew his heart and dealt with him. Many people stop when God deals with them and that's why they never move from that frustration. He had a defining moment with Jesus that changed his ways and his life forever.

I think about Mary with the alabaster box. So much was going on around her, but she too, recognized the moment and took advantage of it. She got His attention by taking what was costly to her and precious. She broke it and she poured it on His feet. When was the last time you didn't ask Him for anything, but just took what was precious to you and gave it to Him? I think in this day and age, that would be our time more than anything else. The enemy will use everything he can to distract us.

I love the story about the woman who touched the hem of His garment. Many probably thought she was crazy. There were so many people there and around Jesus, but He knew something was different. Persistent women get what they want! He felt her faith. She was beyond what others thought. When was the last time you did something that got His attention in a room full of other needs? He responds to persistent women. There was a desperation in her that day and she knew if she could just touch the hem of His garment, she knew she would be made whole. I know someone is reading this right now and you feel God tugging at your heart. Why don't you just stop right now and talk to Him? He's listening...

Just like many others in the Bible. The Bible is full of people who messed up, ran from God and much more. We all have issues we have to work on. He even knew that before we were born and He still decided to create each one of us. Now that's a great Father! Just think – He knew all of that and created us, loved us and has never given up on us. Who are we to say we want to quit? He has never looked for perfect vessels. He has always been searching for faith and willingness. I think it is insulting to God when we say or think He could never forgive us or use us because of our sins or mistakes. That would be like telling Him that what He did on the cross was all in vain. He is a loving God. He is a forgiving God and He is pleased when He knows we are giving it our best.

Your best may look different than another's best. That's why this book has so much about not comparing yourself to others. Your lane is different. It's like two people taking an awesome trip. One is going through the cold mountains to get to their destination and the other is going through the hot desert for their destination. If the one going through the mountains packs just like the one headed through the desert, they are in big trouble. When you are headed in one direction, it is very important what and who you bring with you. A lot of people find themselves stranded because God never told them to take certain paths. People love to say, 'God said so,' when He had nothing to do with it. God doesn't change His mind. We do. We have to stop running every time we get offended or someone corrects us or questions what we think we have heard. These are the moments that really count. God will always speak to the leaders over you and then it's up to you to listen and obey. There's a lot of dead ends where there is no obedience. I think you get the picture I'm painting here. Both places are important and so are the people getting there, but when we start doing things outside of His timing or will, we alter our destiny.

Allow God to mold you during the defining moments of your life. Trauma and let downs do not dictate you, they just define your story and testimony. Instead of hiding what you have been through, make it work for you. Fear will numb you. Jealousy will trap you. Insecurities will shut you down. Doubt will steal your vision. Having no confidence will rob you and hold you hostage.

Remember, whoever has your ear, has your destiny. That's not just talking about God or the devil. That means whoever is pouring into you, has your ear. Surround yourself with radical believers that push you into your destiny.

I want to encourage you to stay in the fight. My grandmother would always tell me to put my horse blinders on and keep my focus. Don't get distracted in the race. Life hits hard sometimes and it's okay to be flawed. Just know that greater is He that is within you than he that is in the world. When life hits you, hit back, bounce back and move forward. The Bible says to count it all joy when various trials come your way. I know, that one doesn't make sense to me either, but it's been proven true over and over again. God promises to never leave us nor forsake us. We may be thrown in the fire, but we are coming out with no smoke! Believe in yourself! You can do ALL things through Christ who gives you strength. We must fully rely on Him and remember not to take on life in our own strength. Let whatever you are walking through right now be a defining moment for you. It could be the very thing that changes your life forever. Respond and act however you want the outcome to be.

LETTER FROM THE FIRST LADY

Fancy hats, 2-piece suits, fancy cars, sometimes loud, sometimes quiet, always on parade. These are just a few things people think of when they see the words 'First Lady'. We have stereotyped so many women that are considered our 'Spiritual Moms'.

Let me speak for myself on this matter. I was raised in a pastor's home for 21 years then married, but still a pastor's daughter and now I have been a Co/Senior Pastor since I was 31 years old. No offense to those who love it, but personally, I have never liked being called 'First Lady'. Our church is well aware of this. We have a running joke that I'm the ONLY lady in my house because if there is a first then there may be a second or third. Not in my house! We laugh, but it's true. No, I am not against anyone being called that, I would just rather not be called that myself.

Some females are married to pastors, or in full time ministry and don't want anything to do with the pulpit or leading in the church. That's okay too, if that is an understanding between their marriage and ministry. For some of us, we love being right in the middle of everything in the ministry. We love ministering right beside our husbands and we know God has ordained us to do so.

The thing I really want to address in this chapter is embracing that female either way. The pressures are great! A lot of times you are judged if you are involved and judged if you are not. To drive the point in this chapter, I will address this role as 'First Lady'.

Many "First Ladies" wake up for church, week after week and the moment their feet hit the ground to get dressed, they start feeling the pressure. The pressure to have the kids looking and acting their best or what to wear. I'll put this outfit on because I love it and it's me, but will they judge me? Will they think I'm too fancy? Will they think I look too fashionable for church? What exactly is a 'First Lady' supposed to look like? As soon as I walk on the stage or to my seat, what will they think? What does my husband need from me today? Am I being all he needs? I can't forget to be in intercession for him too. Let me just put this mask on and no one will ever know.

She walks in and bam! Lights, camera, action! What does

she have on? What will she say today? Does she say enough? Too much? Oh, it doesn't matter anyway because she's just the 'First Lady'... 'pastor's wife'. Let's make sure we take care of him! What people fail to realize is that a huge percentage of those ladies give their lives for their families and for their church and they go unnoticed and forgotten. A lot of prayers are answered because she was the helpmate she was assigned to be. Now, don't think this is self-serving and for me. Let me explain. I have the most AMAZING husband that stood his ground many years ago to let everyone know that we were in this thing together. We copastor together. He is a very confident and strong leader. I love submitting to him because I know he is follower of Christ and we are going in the same direction. He doesn't try to prove any of his manliness by talking down to me, but instead, he empowers me. A woman doesn't have a problem respecting a man when she feels loved and celebrated. My husband is my biggest supporter and I am his. I am also privileged to have a mom that has been full time in ministry as a Co-Pastor with my dad for over forty years. I watched her literally go through hell for many of those years. Thank God that I also have an amazing father that supports her. She is strong and highly anointed. She has shown me many things through example and not just words. She showed me what it looked like to see my enemy on the ground instead of in my face! It might have taken a little while, but I got it!

I just have a big heart for "First Ladies" because I know many of them feel like they are dying inside and no one cares. They feel drained, forgotten and misunderstood. If you are a "First Lady" and you are reading this thinking, *I don't feel this way*, then this chapter may not be for you. I am standing up and speaking for the ones who lay their lives down every day and don't want to say how they really feel. I talk to many that are screaming, "I WANT TO QUIT!" We have to do better as humans, Christians and congregations to treat them like they deserve. Are all perfect? NO! Do some of them flaunt, live ungodly and act like heathens? YES! But again, I am speaking of the ones who are silent storms on your behalf. The ones that pray for you every day. The ones that hurt every time someone leaves the church, good or bad. They love without restraint. They serve when no one is looking. They protect the house you worship in and count it an honor.

I once heard a 'First Lady' say that she went to minister with her husband at an event and they brought him a glass goblet of water and gave her a Styrofoam cup. Can you tell me what's wrong with this picture? When was the last time you told your "First Lady" you appreciated her? Sowed a seed into her life? Brought her a gift card to get her nails done? Just the simple things that remind her that someone is watching and cares. See, so many people are so twisted in their thinking. They see blessed people and miss opportunities to sow into them or bless them because they view it as they are already blessed and don't need it. Maybe they don't need the blessing as much as you need to sow it for yourself. This may sound strong, but it's true and someone needs to speak up and say it. People who are givers never go lacking. It's the ones who never sow that are always begging. He gives seed to the sower. If you are not a sower, that may be why you don't have seed.

Take some time to pray for your "First Lady", "Pastors Wife", "Senior Pastor". She will appreciate it. If you have one that doesn't sound like the description in this chapter, begin to pray for her. Insecure females are only acting out from a root issue. Just remember, it is not your place to ever bring correction. That is her husband and God's job.

Thanks for listening...I hope many are enlightened and we begin to see many more celebrated instead of judged. Don't judge a book by its cover. You never know the trials one is facing.

PASTOR OF ALABASTER

Silence filled the room
But yet something was heard.
Before the shattered box,
Before she spoke a word.

Walking toward Jesus
She understood His pain
Of doing kingdom work but
Being in a room and still just being a name...
Not in it really for the fame.

This would be and is
The parallels between
A woman with alabaster
And a woman pastor.

As she's not just a number,
A digit you will see
Her perfume lasts
Much longer than her visit.
She is a pastor!

To the man, they say....
'But you preach the word...
That's utterly absurd."
She preaches more than I do,
Sometimes it just can't be heard....

They say to the man
"Take this water in a crystal glass
while we give her the Styrofoam.
Our eyes are on you sir..."
While she heads on home...
But what you fail to realize
That's not just a woman...
That's bone of my bone...
My covenant with her
Is with God alone.

Just like Abraham and Sarah...
Both of their names got changed in the covenant...
You can't acknowledge one without her.

'But biblically she's the weaker vessel,'
But no one more than me
Knows the strength of her

Spiritual muscle and spiritual hustle.

She's not JUST a wife of the pastor,
Or simply first lady...the significant other...
While we celebrate the man
The woman stays undercover, smothered.

It's not the title it's the right
Because what she does like me
She does with all of her might,
Even if she wasn't
The speaker of the night.

Pastor's wife sounds like the sidekick,
First lady may mean there's another...
But that's like calling her a sister
When actually she's a mother.

She's more than a pastor's wife
Or a first lady
She's a warrior and a pastor...
Not just a side of gravy

See we are one ...ONE

I can't do without her
The strength she speaks to me
When no one is around,
You don't hear that sound...

She pours out alabaster
And anoints the room with prayer and intercession
Her silence and tears for the ministry
Is the true lesson
If she preaches or not...
She still deserves the blessing...
She's pouring too....
Actually, she pours more than me...
More than you.

But in some places, that's not enough
For her to sit on the stage
She has to stay on the floor....
It's true...
But yet she still pours and pours.

While everyone is in the room
She gives her all as a pastor...
She is magnificent, you see

Just like the woman
With the alabaster.

Others don't credit your labor
'Give her share to the poor
But with Jesus she has found favor
Her life to Him is a sweet-smelling savor.

Just like the woman with the alabaster box...
You might unknowingly deny
Her position and presence...
But you cannot deny her price.
The value to her was given
By JESUS that night...

BE YOU ON PURPOSE…THE MOVEMENT

BYOP BOUTIQUE

A unique boutique that offers a very peaceful atmosphere. Eclectic in style with a bohemian, vintage touch. There are plenty of unique gifts, clothing, jewelry, home goods and much more. Enter the large dressing room and leave a prayer request in the mailbox. There is something for every girl and woman in your life, including you.

Online store website:
www.beyouonpurpose.com
Shop our exclusive lines here.

BYOP FOUNDATION

The BYOP Foundation gives back to all ages and walks of life. One of the dreams is to have a subdivision for single moms and their children that would be offered for a lower price to help them get on their feet and set them up for success. We also give to numerous teens and college-age students. Our heart is big with lots of vision.

Dot, our hippie van, is also part of our foundation. We have 'pop up worship' at different locations, we give out food and water at different events or just set up in random places and give back. Our van also shows up at our Annual BYOP Women's Experience. She is loved and makes a great photo prop!

We also have lots of giveaways that we purchase for the BYOPE (see below). We love giving back!

You can be a part of blessing others by going to www.beyouonpurposefoundation.com and making a tax-deductible donation at any time.

BYOP EXPERIENCE

Our annual teen girl and women's event. This event is held every year and it changes so many lives for the better. We spend a weekend together as we laugh, cry, bond, worship and much more. Visit our BYOPE website for more information on the awesome event.
www.beyouonpurposeexperience.com

Made in the USA
Middletown, DE
14 May 2017